PSYCHE:

A PRIZE ESSAY

ON THE

IMMATERIALITY OF THE MIND

AND THE

IMMORTALITY OF THE SOUL;

THE PROOFS AND PRESUMPTIONS THEREOF DEDUCED FROM
THE LIGHT OF NATURE AND REASON,
APART FROM REVELATION.

BY J. A. LEATHERLAND.

"To be, or not to be, that is the question."

SHAKESPERE.

NORTHAMPTON: PRINTED BY JAS. BUTTERFIELD;
AND MAY BE HAD OF THE BOOKSELLERS, WELLINGBOROUGH
AND KETTERING, OR OF THE AUTHOR.
1853.

DEDICATION.

TO THE REV. T. H. MADGE, M.A.,

RECTOR OF KETTERING,

These pages are very respectfully dedicated, as a humble but sincere tribute of gratitude for his kindness to the Author during a long and severe affliction.

Kettering, Nov. 1st, 1853.

PREFACE.

Some months since, A. Robertson, Esq., M.D., kindly offered to the Members of the Northamptonshire Religious and Useful Knowledge Society, Prizes for the two best Essays on "The Immateriality of the Mind and the Immortality of the Soul; the proofs and presumptions thereof deduced from the light of Nature and Reason, apart from Revelation." Seven Essays were sent in for adjudication, distinguished by their respective signatures, when the Adjudicators unanimously awarded the first prize to the writer of the Essay bearing the motto "Hope," * and the second to the one subscribed "Zetetes," and recommended both as worthy of publication. In submitting this, the second of these Essays, to the public notice, its Author begs for the candour of his readers, inasmuch as it is the first time that he has solicited their attention, and also as he is a humble artisan, who has been denied the advantages of an education now happily enjoyed by almost every schoolboy. The composition of the following pages greatly relieved the tedium of an illness which was, in some respects, an advantage, as it afforded leisure to pursue the subject, which he could not otherwise have obtained. Perhaps this small pamphlet may be read by some who cannot afford time, or who have not sufficient resolution to study, the more voluminous or abstruse metaphysical writers upon this important subject. Should this humble effort be of the least service in checking the specious infidelity of the age, it will afford its author high satisfaction. He greatly doubts

* Written by Mr. B. Simpson, of Northampton, and since published. I have read it with much interest. J. A. L.

whether he has treated in an original manner subjects which have already been so much discussed, but begs to state that he is not conscious of any plagiarism or imitation. Upon these topics coincident ideas spontaneously arise in the mind of every thinking person; and their very spontaneity and universality would seem to furnish an argument in favour of their truth.

To the Donor, the Adjudicators, and the Author's numerous and influential Friends who have subscribed towards this publication, he tenders his sincere thanks.

Kettering, Nov. 1st, 1853.

ARGUMENT.

Introduction—The excellency of Man's Mental Nature—His performances—These interrupted by Death—Does the Soul survive that event?—Definitions of the terms "Mind" and "Soul"—How spoken of by the Ancients—How understood by us—God the archetype of the Human Soul—Differences between Man and the Brute—The properties of Mind and Matter contrasted—Mind not the result of Material organization—On Personal Identity—The proof of the Immateriality of the Mind a strong argument for its Immortality—Other proofs—The Providence of God—The endowments and aspirations of the Soul—Conclusion.

PSYCHE: A PRIZE ESSAY.

The nature and destiny of the Mind or Soul of man, comprehending those sublime faculties which distinguish him from all other sentient creatures of which he is cognizant, is surely a subject of the first importance, and of the most intense interest.

No sooner does his Reason expand her powers, and Imagination plume her wing—no sooner does his Mind develop its nature and begin to *think*—than he finds himself substantially related to those mighty Intelligences who have subdued the stubborn elements to their will; who have scaled the summits of the earth, explored its depths, navigated its seas, analyzed its matter, defined its figure, size and motions, tamed and brought into servitude its inferior animals; and who, in short, by the force of their mental powers, exerted over inert and organized nature, have won for themselves, beyond dispute, the glorious title of the "Lords of the Creation."

And, if he turn from the triumphs of his race over what is merely physical,* to consider their nobler and more ideal achievements, he finds more admirable proofs of his sublime capacities. The glowing canvas, the graceful statue, the marvellous edifice, the graphic history, the subtle disquisition, the immortal poem—are all

---

* I have used the term "physical" throughout these pages in the sense of material or corporeal, in opposition to that which is mental or spiritual. I believe it is popularly so used, but such use is not strictly correct, as there is the physics of the mind. The word is derived from the Greek φυσιχος (phusixos)—natural, innate, in opposition to artificial.

so many trophies which attest the dignity of his species, and—swelling his soul with noble aspiration—invite him to lofty emulation. And, although there are comparatively few who possess this creative or delineative faculty (which is termed genius), and the number who can appreciate these intellectual works—though much greater—even in civilized nations is small indeed, yet there is scarcely an individual who at all exercises his mental faculties who is not, at one time or other, startled at his own powers; whose imagination does not launch out into the infinite, whose thoughts do not strive to lay hold on the eternal; whose emotions are not too big for utterance, who does not feel himself to be indeed fearfully and wonderfully endowed.

And yet how humiliating is the fact, that the whole human family, in common with the meanest thing that breathes, must bow to a mysterious and inevitable law that interferes with all their designs, and terminates all their operations!—that, by disease and death, their fairest plans are frustrated, their grandest attempts rendered abortive, and their dearest wishes disappointed!—that the eye of the astronomer, which pierces into the depths of the firmament, must be quenched in darkness, and the brain of the philosopher, which resolves the profoundest problems, must moulder into common dust!—that the strain of the poet must cease, and his tongue be hushed in the silence of death!—that all who live must die—the sage and the idiot, the renowned and the obscure! It becomes, then, a question of the greatest consequence—What is the mental nature of man, and how will death affect it? Has he an immaterial Spirit, destined to survive the dissolution of the body, and then enter into another state of existence; or, are his mental powers (as the materialist would urge) merely the result of his physical organization, converging in the brain, and there developing themselves, but which must necessarily be dependent upon that organ for their manifestation, and cease to act whenever its mechanism is destroyed?

It will be my endeavour in these pages, very briefly, to prove the truth of the theory involved in the former of these questions, viz., that man possesses an immaterial, immortal principle; and, in conformity with the conditions proposed, I shall confine myself to discussing it from Nature and Reason alone, apart from Revelation.

But, before proceeding, it may perhaps, be necessary, in order to prevent confusion, to define the meaning of the terms "MIND" and "SOUL", as used in the title of this Essay. I conceive that they are not meant to denote distinct existences or essences, but that they both refer to the same principle, and that the distinction is only made in relation to its different manifestations, and the agreement of the words with the nouns-adjective to which they are joined.

The ancient Greek philosophers employed three terms to denote the vital and mental principle. First, Zoe (Ζυη), or Zo (Ζω) signifying life or animation, which was used in common to designate the vitality of men and brutes; secondly, Pneuma (Πνευμα), signifying breath or respiration, and, in a higher sense, by later writers, the spirit or soul; and, thirdly, Psuche (ψυχη), often expressive of an image of the soul (afterwards deified by the Latin Mythologists as Psyche), and spoken of by Homer* as a departed spirit, by Demosthenes and Sophocles† more abstractedly as the seat of the understanding, by Isocrates as the disposition, or the seat of the passions, or feeling; by others as a living being, a man; and often as a term of endearment, as phile psuche (φιλη ψυχη), "dear soul"; and it was also employed to denote a moth or butterfly, from the beautiful transformation of those insects affording a type of the soul and its higher nature in a future state.

Amongst ourselves, the term "Mind" is used in popular language to express the *thinking* faculty, and "Soul" the *emotional.* Thus, we say the Mind wills, perceives, or reflects; the Soul feels, loves, or abhors. The Mind judges, reasons, distinguishes; the Soul suffers and enjoys, grieves and rejoices, desires and dreads. The Mind, as so designated, may be compared to the depths of the ocean—calm, vast and unfathomable; and the Soul to the surface of that ocean—changeful, tossed by storms, and troubled by interrupting agencies, or smiling in tranquil beauty and reflecting the image of heaven. Still it is the same ocean in both cases, and so we apprehend the thinking and emotional faculties are both, but different, manifestations of the same essence,—both constituting that grand principle of the nature of man wherein consists his mental identity.

For it were difficult to perceive how that identity could be preserved in man if he were a duplex being—if, in fact, he has two distinct mental natures which are not referable to one common essence—any more than the Siamese twins could constitute one individual. I propose, therefore, to use these words in their common acceptation, as referring to the mental nature of man, and shall endeavour to prove that that mental nature is a single, incorporeal, immortal essence.

The first argument I would adduce in proof of the Immateriality of the Mind is afforded by considering the nature of the Deity, and tracing the analogy which exists between God *as a spirit*, and the *spirit* of man.

Of course neither the Atheist nor the Pantheist will admit this reasoning. The man that disbelieves in the existence of the Deity,

---

* Iliad. Book 23. Ver. 65.
† Sophocles. Elect. 775.

and he that only regards Him as a being identical with nature, will deny the major of this proposition, viz., that there exists an Infinite Spirit at all; consequently to such objectors the inference would have no weight. But all who believe that there exists an almighty, omnipresent, infinite, eternal Being, from whom all other being proceeds,—who pervades nature and encompasses it, yet exists independently of, and apart from, it,—do, I think, grant *that* from which inferences may be deduced which tend to prove the immateriality of the Mind of man. For, I would observe, the nature of the Deity must be immaterial. If the existence of a God is admitted at all, it is surely absurd to suppose Him a physical being resembling ourselves—a vast Titan, moving from place to place, superintending the spheres as we might superintend an orrery or a workshop. Then, however vast he might be, he could only be in one place at a time; there would be bounds to his presence, and all outside that presence must exist apart from him, and be near to, or remote from, his influence. Then, instead of being omnipresent, he would be a mere *genius loci;* whereas throughout nature we receive abundant hints of His ubiquity and His pervading influence. But this point need not further be discussed. If there be one thing that Natnre teaches more plainly than another it is that, if there be a God, that God is an immaterial being. He is not cognizant to the senses, yet His presence is universally felt; —the star and the daisy, the sun and the sunflower, the ocean and the dewdrop, the hughest and the most minute formations, with organized life in its multifarious forms, in short, every thing that surrounds us, as well as we ourselves, attest the presence of a great invisible Spirit—

> "Who gives its lustre to an insect's wing,
> And wheels his flight upon the rolling worlds."

From what the light of Nature reveals of the attributes of this great Spirit, I think that He is shewn therein as the Archetype, as He is the Author, of the human Soul, and differs from it more in the degree and perfection of those attributes than in their kind. Nay, farther, that there is a greater radical difference in this latter respect between man and the brute than between man and God. It is true that, as mechanical agents, the inferior animals exhibit wonderful instances of sagacity and skill. The cell of the bee, the nest of the bird, and the storehouse of the ant, have in every age been regarded as admirable examples of contrivance, and perfect specimens of the best adaptation of means to the end designed. But this very *precision* seems to intimate that they are instinctively, and, in a sense, passively, obeying the dictates of an unerring law, rather than acting as intelligent, thinking, reflecting beings. Apart from what they are impulsively led to do by their own instinctive powers, their actions betray little that is intellectual. There are no fresh developments*, no strange discoveries, no mental suggestions, no aspiring endeavours : all is tame, precise, stereotyped, calculable, monotonous, *after their kind*, beautifully adapted for the state in which they exist, but showing or hinting nothing beyond. The human Soul, on the contrary, both in its mental and moral constitution, reflects, though dimly and imperfectly, the nature of the Deity. In the intellectual efforts and achievements of man ; in his sublime aspirations ; in his longings after the infinite ; in his vague desires and anticipations ; in his power, his skill, his wisdom, his sympathies, his understanding ; his sense of justice, of propriety, of virtue ; in his love of beauty and hatred of deformity ;— in short, in all those things that make up the excellency of his nature, he appears to approximate towards his Divine Original, and faintly shadow His glorious perfections. May not we, then, justly conclude that, as is the archetype so is the type ; as is the sun so is the spark ;—that, if nature abundantly manifests the existence of a spiritual being of the highest order, other beings of kindred, though inferior, powers partake of a nature essentially similar in its kind ? This analogy between the greater and the less may be traced throughout the creation. Indeed, it is the only method of judging and proving the nature of those things which we cannot grasp, or submit to the test of the senses or of experiment. Thus Franklin inferred that electricity and lightning were identical, before he demonstrated the fact by drawing it from the clouds. Thus the chemist takes a small quantity of common air and analyzes it, and from it deduces the nature of the atmosphere. In like manner he takes a drop of water, and from it proves the nature of the ocean. By this method, also, the natural philosopher classifies and arranges the various objects that exist according to the corresponding similitudes or properties which he discovers in them. Thus, too, the peasant who has never seen the ocean, or any greater collection of waters than a pool or small lake, while viewing its miniature phenomena—its tiny billows tossed by the wind, its feeble surges

---

* I cannot refrain here from quoting the following beautiful passage from the poet Montgomery upon this subject :—

> " The nightingale which sung in Adam's bower,
> " And pour'd her stream of music through his dreams ;—
> " The soaring lark that led the eye of Eve
> " Into the clouds————
> " The dove that perch'd upon the tree of life,
> " And made her nest amongst its thickest boughs ;—
> " All the wing'd inhabitants of Paradise,
> " Whose songs were mingled with the songs of angels—
> " Built their first nests as curiously and well
> " As the wood minstrels of our latest day."

PELICAN ISLAND.

beating against the banks, or its surface, when not disturbed or polluted, imaging the trees that grow upon its side, or the firmament that hangs above it—is convinced that the unknown, unexplored deep is analogous in its nature, although, from what he has heard of it, it is so vastly superior in its manifestations.

May not, then, the inference be fairly drawn, that as God is an immaterial Being, judging, contriving, and acting in the most perfect manner, independently of matter, so the mind of man, shewing similar powers, though far more imperfect ones, and possessing a kindred nature, though a far inferior one, (and, alas, how much debased by his own sin and folly!) is immaterial and spiritual also?

Secondly. The Immateriality of the Mind may be shown from the fact that its qualities, or attributes, are totally unlike the properties or qualities of material things, and that they possess nothing in common.

We know nothing, nor can know anything whatever, of the substratum or essence of any substance, but pronounce on its nature according to the properties or attributes that belong to it. Now, the properties or qualities of matter are of two kinds. First, those that are common, and essential to its nature, which it can never lose, but always retains under every condition, whatever be its transformation, as impenetrability, divisibility, specific gravity and dimension; and, secondly, those that are accidental, which it may retain or lose, according as it is acted upon, as colour, shape, solidity, size; hardness, softness; roughness, smoothness, and so forth. For example: we take a piece of ice, which we all know to be a cold, solid, brittle, transparent substance; we submit it to the action of increased temperature, when it loses the three former of these properties, and we recognise it as a fluid: again, by further heat being applied to it, it is converted into the extremely attenuated and elastic vapour which we call steam; which, by the same agency, may be again changed into its component gases. Yet throughout all these transformations we are sure it is the same essence, though appearing in different states, and under different forms, according to the agency which is brought to bear upon it. This is given as a familiar instance, but examples need not be multiplied. The reader is too well acquainted with the various modifications which all things material are perpetually undergoing, and with their different and opposite qualities, to need further illustration.

Now, in no one of these qualities, whether essential or accidental, does the Soul bear any resemblance to material things. To impute to it any of their properties would be preposterous and absurd. It can neither be weighed, divided nor penetrated, nor has it a tangible form. It is not manifested through the medium of the senses, which is the only way that anything material is made known to us. It has neither colour, solidity or size, or any other of the common properties of matter. Fire, wind and light have, indeed, been sometimes used to furnish representations of it, but merely as poetic tropes, on account of their being subtle and refined in their nature, and the least resembling aught else that is material.

But it must not be supposed that because the Mind possesses no properties in common with matter, that it is, therefore, a mere negation. It has qualities and attributes peculiar to itself, which appear to be the highest manifestations of anything, and the most abiding. I have before hinted at some of these in tracing the analogy between God and the Soul, and would now more specifically mention them. Metaphysicians have classified them in different ways, and Phrenologists have detailed them with minuteness. But it will be sufficient for my purpose if I briefly refer to the most remarkable. These may be summarily comprehended under the three powers of Volition, Perception and Reflection; those of volition being the various acts of the Will, as desiring, choosing, &c.; those of perception of the Senses, as seeing, hearing, &c.; and those of reflection, as remembering, judging, reasoning, &c. Now, it is obvious that these psychological phenomena are totally distinct from, and unlike any, of the qualities or modifications of matter; as is also the fact that, that essence or substance in which they all inhere is simple and not compound, and incapable of division. If, then, the Mind be regarded as material, do not we act in direct opposition to all principles of classification, and blend into one homogeneous compound things which will not coalesce, and place in one catagory those things which nature itself teaches us to distinguish and separate?

But, it may be asked, are we not dependent upon matter for our ideas? And, if so, does not this shew that matter and mind are intimately connected and related?

It has long been a disputed question whether the ideas of the Mind are originally, to some extent, innate, or whether they are all derived through the medium of the senses. I do not intend to enter upon this discussion, for it must be allowed that, if the former theory be the true one, the number of such innate ideas is very limited: but I think that this is attributable to the circumscribed state in which the Mind is placed, rather than to its capacity; that it is because it is confined to this medium of action, rather than because it is unable to act otherwise. In like manner the palate may, owing to circumstances, be confined to tasting only an inferior and coarse kind of diet, but it is quite capable of relishing different and richer food if such be provided. So the eye of a prisoner is able to take in only a very few objects, and it may be those of the tamest kind, from the loop-holes of his cell; but certainly not because of the incapacity of his vision, but on account of his view being thus limited. Fling down his prison walls or remove him to an eminence, and his sight will range far and wide, among beauties and sublimities before unknown.

The high and active properties of the Mind are also shown by the very ingenious manner in which its primitive ideas are combined by the aid of the fancy, or imagination, until they appear as original conceptions: and also by the reasonings, deductions and inferences which the Mind is able to draw from whatever is presented to it. And certainly the feelings and emotions of the Soul often seem to rise above material objects altogether. Language is too poor to express them, and affords no medium to convey them to other Minds, and no symbol with which to compare them. They are unearthly, unutterable and divine. How often, too, is the body found to be a clog to the soul, and the senses an hindrance to its contemplations! So far from assisting it in its highest thoughts, they only distract and divert it; for it is found that those who are the most attracted by them, and the most eager for their gratification, are amongst the most degraded; while those who abstain as much as possible from sensual pleasures and desires make the most progress in that which is intellectual. So also is it found that those who have lost the use of one or more of the senses, find such loss no obstacle to the exertion of their mental powers: of this there are many notable examples, for every one must allow that Homer, Galileo and Milton thought to purpose without their sight.

We find, therefore, that although the Mind is indebted to sensual or material objects, as furnishing images to supply it with a store of ideas; or, to change the figure, as giving it food to ruminate or digest, it is not dependent upon them for its power of acting, neither does it shew any affinity to them in its nature.

Thirdly. The Mind and its phenomena are not referable to material organization.

It is a favourite hypothesis with the Materialist that mental phenomena are the result of this organization. It has been already noticed that the highest manifestations of Mind, namely, those of the Deity, are not shewn in connection with such organization. Why, then, should the human Mind result from it? The various contrivances of man, and the different combinations and appliances of his skill, have produced many admirable and surprising results; yet from all the numerous machines which he has constructed, nothing analogous to thought has been developed, unless, indeed, the ingenious calculating apparatus of Babbage may be held to furnish an instance.

The Materialist says it is the *brain* that thinks; that this is its specific function in the same way as the eye sees and the ear hears. I reply, exactly so: but every physiologist admits that the *eye* does not see; that the *ear* does not hear *per se*, but that they are only *instruments* for the conveying of these sensations to the brain or Mind. No one believes that a telescope sees, or an ear trumpet hears, yet these are only artificial contrivances for extending these senses. We may use them or lay them aside, but the *capacity* remains, and this capacity, in common with other powers of perception, resides in the Mind. If, then, the eye or the ear be only agents or instruments of sensation, why should the brain be regarded as more than the agent or instrument of thought? Can it be the agent and the cause also? If the senses are referable to the brain, must not the brain be referable to something to which *it* also acts as an instrument? If the faculty of vision does not reside in the eye, why should it be supposed that that of thought resides in the brain? The Phrenologist has divided that organ into many distinct, and, I think, somewhat fanciful, partitions, to each of which he assigns specific powers; but supposing this science to be correct in all its minuteness, it only proves that the soul employs a compound instrument instead of a simple one.

A familiar illustration may be given of this. A pianoforte has been beautifully called "a piece of furniture with a soul in it;" but we never suppose the different keys or strings of that instrument to constitute its *music*. That is referable to a higher, a more ethereal substance, the strings or keys only supplying the medium of action. So the different organs of the brain convey to the Mind the impressions made upon them by the world without, and produce those mental effects which may be compared to harmony. And this very naturally accounts for the fact, so strongly dwelt upon by the Materialist, that as the faculties of the body develop themselves, so the mental powers grow stronger, as well as usually decline with its debility and decay. I say *usually*, for there are exceptions sufficient to shew that the Mind does not always correspond with the body in this respect, which must be the case if it were material. But it is generally so found; shewing that, when the latter is deranged or weakened, it acts in like manner upon the former, as a musical instrument, when broken or worn out, brings forth only feeble or discordant sounds.

But it may be objected that matter being visible, or palpable, declares its existence more fully than spirit. But to what is it thus visible or palpable? To itself? Is it matter that thus sees and feels as well as that which is thus seen or felt? To allow this were to reason in a circle—to confound the agent with the subject—that which perceives and knows with that which is perceived and known.

We have more evidence of the existence of Spirit than of Matter; the latter is only made known to us by the perception of the senses, which is sometimes delusive; but the former by consciousness, which is the most satisfactory of all evidence. It is, indeed, curious that any one should doubt the existence of that principle by which he attains the knowledge of the being of any other, and appears as absurd as for a mathematician to doubt the self-evident axioms upon which the whole of his demonstrations rest.

Fourthly. Another proof of the Immateriality of the Mind is afforded by its identity through all the changes of the physical system.

It is not necessary to enter into any metaphysical discussion for the purpose of proving this identity. We are all convinced of the fact. Our consciousness attests it, and our memory furnishes evidences of it. The man who has lived for fifty or sixty years knows that he is the same person that he was in youth, in childhood, or in infancy. He can recollect the events of his former life, and never doubts that those events pertain to him as the same individual. Yet it is an ascertained fact that his entire bodily structure has repeatedly changed during that period. There is not a particle of the same matter in his brain, or his heart, or his blood, that there was twenty years back. It is true the change has been very gradual, but it is on that account no less complete. Suppose that from a gallon of sand only one grain be abstracted every hour, and another one placed in its stead, it must be evident that at a given period the whole mass would be as completely changed as if it were done at once. Nor must we confound the resemblance with the identity. It is true the fresh particles of matter are, so to speak, placed in the same mould. The man may retain similar features, a similar gait, a similar tone of voice, &c., (yet in the course of time these peculiarities often greatly alter,) but this resemblance no more constitutes his identity than the successive impressions of a printed book constitute it the same copy. Is it not evident, then, that, if identity does not reside in the Body, it must reside in the Mind?—that there must be something which these corporeal changes do not affect?—an entity that the finger of Time cannot abstract or touch?—that he cannot take away a particle of thought, an atom of will, a molecule of judgment, or a globule of imagination, although he changes the brain piecemeal, and, in a few years, alters the entire bodily man? This argument may be briefly shewn in the following double syllogism:—

That which is changed (whether at once or gradually) cannot remain the same.

But the entire body is imperceptibly changed.

Therefore it is not the same as before that change.

But the Mind being the same is unchanged.

But all that is corporeal (*i.e.*, material) is changed, *ergo*, the Mind must be immaterial.

Did not my limits forbid, I might gather up other evidence in proof of the Immateriality of the Mind, such as the phenomena of sleep and dreaming, the general belief in supernatural agency, and other kindred topics, but must desist; nor should I have dwelt so long upon this part of my subject, did not I consider that proofs of the immateriality of our mental nature tell strongly in favour of its immortality also.

For if the Soul be an incorporeal essence, the decay and death of the body will, not destroy but, release it; and if sensation reside in it, in common with its other faculties, it will then no longer have to act through a medium which is often blunted and imperfect, but it will be "all eye, all ear, all sense;" perceiving at once those objects of which it is now only dimly and feebly cognizant.

But it must be allowed that the Creator of both matter and spirit could, if he saw fit, annihilate the soul at any moment, even if it be immaterial; while on the contrary He could continue in perpetual existence matter itself; and so far as our observation goes He does so continue it; for decay and dissolution must not be confounded with annihilation, or a tendency towards it. Every organized being undergoes a process of gradual development, maturity, decay and dissolution; but this dissolution only precedes fresh forms of life, which, in their turn, undergo the same change. Still we think Reason would deduce a termination of being (as far as identity is concerned) from the materiality of the Mind; while the fact of its immateriality—not of necessity sharing the death of the body—furnishes a strong presumptive proof of its surviving that event, and existing for ever.

For I need scarcely stop to remark that the future existence of the soul may be considered as the pledge and promise of its immortality. It is not to be supposed that God, who is unchangeable, should create a soul, and endow it with faculties which are constantly progressing, and powers capable of ever-growing enjoyment, yet capriciously, at some given moment, annihilate it. I can discover or conceive of no motive for this in His character as a moral governor, or as an all-wise Being; and, as it has been before stated, nothing is known in the operations of nature anything like annihilation at all. I submit, then, that it may be taken for granted,—what few who believe in a future state of existence will be inclined to dispute,—that, if the Soul exist in a future state, such existence will endure for ever.

On the doctrine of the Immortality of the Soul I need not dwell at length. The subject has often been ably and eloquently discussed. The man is to be pitied whose mind is not convinced, and whose soul is not warmed, by the brilliant pages of those who have discoursed upon this sublime theme,—by the glowing fervour of Jeremy Taylor, the classic beauties of Addison, the logical arguments of Butler, the sententious poetry of Young, or the philosophical speculations of Drew or Dick. Such great and gifted minds have lifted to the imagination the veil which shrouds the invisible world from the sense, and have given us "glimpses that oft make us less forlorn" while we are imprisoned in this fleshly tabernacle.

The providence of God furnishes a strong argument for the Soul's immortality.

In this world how often are the workings of Providence dark and mysterious! The events which have transpired since the earliest period of history have fully borne out the saying of the inspired Observer, "His ways are in the seas, and His footsteps are not known." How often has the poet lamented the depression of virtue, and the triumph of vice! How do worth and goodness pine in obscurity, while the sordid, the sensual and the selfish are reckoned among the Gods of the earth! How does the independent and deserving mind have to buffet with the difficulties and woes of life, while the worthless and the vile often bask in prosperity and ease! In what inextricable confusion are human affairs often found! How does death appear to be no respecter of persons; or, if he do seem to choose his victims, how often are they among the most worthy, the most useful, or the best beloved! Although we think there is far less inequality in reality than in appearance in the condition of mankind; that there is a compensating principle in nature which, in no small degree, makes up for the privations and depressions of fortune; and that Providence is often charged with the evils which are entailed by the follies or vices of men; yet it does appear to require a wider area, and a longer period, to work out its comprehensive scheme and its vast results. Take away the idea of a future state from suffering humanity, and you deprive the sufferer of his greatest panacea, of his chief support; of that which makes his present calamity tolerable, of that hope which is the best antidote to the cup of bitterness which he is obliged to drink! You add ten-fold to the miseries which encompass him! You extinguish the only gleam of light which shines into the darkness that surrounds him! You increase immensely the difficulties of his position, and efface those divine characters of justice and moral government which are written on every heart! But if at death he is to emerge from this state of privation, suffering and sorrow, and put on the robes of immortality, the very calamities which he has undergone in this transitory state will add immensely to his felicity. The very contrast will give a keener zest to his enjoyment; and this would appear to be one high reason for the permission of evil at all. Every one knows how sweet health is after sickness, and ease after pain: how a compensation is almost afforded for the sufferings endured. The virtuous will then comprehend why they were made to taste of the bitter waters of life, and why it was a state of probation; while they will be far more able to appreciate the happiness to which they have attained than if they had never suffered at all. The view, too, of the operations of Providence will be greatly extended. Now only a small segment of the vast circle is visible—the majestic proportions of the plan are lost by the narrow range of the mental vision; but duration and infinity will be for ever unfolding it more fully, and for ever making it more intelligible to the soul!

Again. The capacities, desires and aspirations of man require a future life for their full completion and satisfaction.

These sublime wishes and anticipations show the true nobility of our nature. They are also instinctive and appear to be given us for the highest purposes.

That man betrays a degraded soul, a coarse and vulgar mind, who is satisfied with present gratifications, and shews no wish beyond them. The highest intellects which have ever appeared seem to have lived in the past and the future, the distant and the ideal; and to have cherished those divine musings, those "thoughts that wander through eternity," which speculate upon and anticipate a future state. It is the belief in this state which makes the emotions caused by the sublime and beautiful to be intelligible and full of meaning. What mean the strange feelings that crowd in upon the soul among Alpine scenery, in the depths of the forest, or within view of the ocean? Why the mysterious awe felt upon walking along the dim aisles of a cathedral, or in listening to the solemn anthem swelling along its arches, or echoing from its lofty roof? What mean the grace and beauty of the unrivalled Venus dé Medicis—"the statue that enchants the world"? Why do we linger over the magnificent paintings of Raphael, or Guido, or Titian? Why does the tragedy of Macbeth make the hair stand on end, or Hamlet fill the soul with unutterable thoughts? Why are we "never merry when we hear sweet music"? or why does it bear us away as on a seraph's wing? These are all intimations of a nobler, a more spiritual life, pointing onward and upward to it, and chiefly valuable for the suggestions they afford; and if this life is not to be realised, they are but dark enigmas! empty delusions! cruel mockeries! sublime nothings! tantalizing deceptions!

Scepticism is adverse to literature as well as to devotion,* and especially is it fatal to Poetry and the Fine Arts. Indeed, I think it impossible for an Atheist to be a Poet in the highest, the truest, sense of that word. It may suit the worldly, plodding utilitarian to be without a religious creed, but this state is far too cold for the warm imagination of the Bard. Were all his hopes and all his prospects to end in the dreary grave, his harp would be robbed of its sweetest string, and his song would be but an idle sound; but it is because he feels that he has within him a principle that will survive the "wreck of matter and the crush of worlds", that he often attunes

---

* Would not the connection between Literature and Religion furnish an interesting subject for an essay?

his lyre in a strain only inferior to that of the angels above, and antedates the employments of the skies. Is it, then, to be supposed that a God of infinite benevolence would endow his creatures with these capacities and desires, and yet fail to gratify them? Does He do this in any other part of His economy? and would He satisfy the meaner portion of His creation and not the nobler? Are not hints given us every night, from the starry firmament above us, of the boundlessness of His resources and the riches of His universe? Why, then should it be doubted that even we may share in this infinity, and enjoy these riches?

And what heart can conceive the felicity that it is possible for the Soul to enjoy when disembodied, and become a denizen of the skies! If we can now look through the crevices of our fleshly prison, and behold so much that is fair and beautiful, how shall we be enraptured when its walls will be thrown down, and we find ourselves amid grander scenes than the warmest fancy had imagined! If we enjoy so much gratification from dipping into the rill of Truth which meanders through this vale of tears, what unutterable felicity must be experienced by being launched out on its pure and broad waters, which will be perpetually widening and deepening through an infinity of ages!

If what I have been endeavouring to prove be true, how great the responsibility it involves! It is a solemn thing to die; it is a serious thing to live. Perhaps that which is the most shocking to the feelings of all right-minded men is the flippant, sneering tone in which sceptics (almost without exception) treat the subject of religion and a future state. Scorn is the cant of infidelity, but it is sadly out of place on such topics, and shows bad taste as well as a depraved heart. Such disputations ought surely to be conducted with gravity, and fair legitimate arguments and appeals to the understanding only be used.

Finally. How thankful ought we to be for the Book of Inspiration, wherein "life and immortality are brought to light"! While endeavouring to pursue this subject by the aid of Reason and the light of Nature alone, the writer felt himself to be groping in the dark, and faintly tracing, in the hieroglyphics of creation, the nature of God and of our own spirits. Neither does he think it possible now to treat this subject altogether apart from the light which Revelation sheds. In reading the opinions of the wisest ancient philosophers as to the nature of the Soul, and its destiny, he was much struck with the whimsical and absurd character of many of their notions. Socrates believed in the pre-existence of the Soul before birth, as well as its transmigration into that of the brute. Plato, too, was of the same opinion. Indeed, this was the creed of all the most celebrated Grecian philosophers. These profound thinkers, not having the light of the Bible to guide them in their investigations, were led astray by the *ignus fatuus* of their own fancy. Not possessing the Oracles of Divine Truth, they could only listen to the voice of their own reason; what wonder, then, that they thus erred! But Inspiration now clears up the doubts that have so long enveloped this mysterious subject, and declares, with the voice of God himself, its important truths.

> "This is the Judge that stints the strife
> Where wit and reason fail"—

Deciding the most embarrassing questions in the simplest manner, and pronouncing the will of God in the plainest words. He that in humility and faith receives this Holy Word, to him will doubtless be given all necessary knowledge; but he that proudly and perversely spurns its teachings will wander farther and farther in the mazes of error and perplexity, bewildered and lost amidst the mysteries of the universe, and shrouded in its gathering gloom.

ZETETES.

June 21st, 1853.

JAS. BUTTERFIELD, PRINTER, NORTHAMPTON.

Milton Keynes UK
Ingram Content Group UK Ltd.
UKHW051052220424
441551UK00011B/955